CHAPTER 1

Anagkazo, Biazo and Anaideia

...Go out into the highways and hedges, and compel [*anagkazo*] them to come in, that my house may be filled.

Luke 14:23

1

What is Anagkazo?

Anagkazo **simply means** *"to compel"*. It also means to *necessitate,* to *drive*, and to *constrain* by all means such as *force*, *threats*, *persuasion* and *entreaties*.

Sometimes we need to go back to the Greek in order to understand the original meanings of some Bible words. You see, the New Testament was translated from the Greek language and the Old Testament from the Hebrew language. Anagkazo is the Greek word that is translated "to compel".

There is another closely related Greek word, *"Biazo"*.

What is Biazo?

Biazo is a Greek word found in Matthew 11 that means *"to use force"* or *"to force one's way into a thing"*. This is a quality I find lacking in Christian circles. We are forceful about everything else, except God's work. We are forceful about our jobs, our girlfriends, our marriages and our future. But when it comes to God's work we become like timid mice!

When I see commercials on television, I realize that there are groups of people who are very confident about what they have to offer. They are so confident that they boldly sing catchy songs about how good their product is.

Alcohol advertisers are some of the best in the business. We all know that beer and liquor are killers and destroyers of young people. Alcohol has broken up more homes, destroyed more marriages, caused more car accidents, and started more wars and fights than anything else in the world. Yet, it is advertised and promoted constantly. Beer is the cause of many accidents, leading to the deaths of countless numbers of people. And yet there are smiling people on television, telling us that it is the "power" we need. These commercials are being forced down our throats. We are being forced to believe things that are not true.

Even though beer is the "devil in solution" we are being compelled to believe otherwise.

When I think of the forcefulness of people who want to make money at all costs, I realize that Christians have a better reason to be forceful. Why then is it that we Christians behave like lame ducks, toothless dogs and helpless sparrows?

I believe that the revelation of *anagkazo* and *biazo* can change that. Biazo means to force one's way into a thing. If Christianity is going to spread we are going to have to be a lot more forceful than we are.

Whether it is making money, spreading a false religion or selling deadly products, the world is forceful about it. That is why I am teaching Christians to be biblically forceful.

What is Anaideia?

Another related Greek word I want us to study is the word "*Anaideia*". *Anaideia* is a Greek word that is used only once in the Bible. It means "*to be shameless*". In the eleventh chapter of Luke, we learn of a man who exhibited shamelessness in his relationship with God.

I say unto you, Though he will not rise and give him, because he is his friend, yet because of his importunity [*anaideia*] he will rise and give him as many as he needeth.

Luke 11:8

In 1982, I was admitted to the University of Ghana, the premier university in my country, Ghana. I cautiously entered this new environment wondering what lay ahead. One of the first things that struck me was the shamelessness of unbelievers.

The Kissing Students

I remember one of the first times I walked into Volta Hall, the ladies' hall. When I got to the staircase that led up to the first and second floors, there was a young man and a girl engaged in a prolonged embrace and kiss. I know that in some places this might not look strange. However it looked strange to me.

This couple continued in their long embrace and intimate kissing as we passed by them. They could not care less about who saw them! They were not moved! They were shameless! Perhaps they felt they were in love.

When we got upstairs, I told my friends, "It seems people around here are not ashamed of what they're doing."

Then I asked, "Why are we ashamed of what we believe in?

Why are we ashamed of the Gospel?

Why do we go around like timid mice that don't have anything to offer?"

The Spirit of the Lord rose up within me and I said, "If they are not ashamed of their immoral lives, I'm not going to be ashamed of the Gospel."

For I am not ashamed of the gospel of Christ...

Romans 1:16

It is amazing to see homosexuals boldly speak of their abnormal lifestyles. They come on television and speak confidently about the anomaly of anal intercourse. These people forcefully demonstrate for their rights. How come Christians are so quiet when it comes to speaking God's Word?

Many Christians sit in their offices and allow their unbeliever colleagues to shamelessly speak of their evil deeds. The sinners around us dominate the discussions with unwholesome words.

The Apostle Paul practised *anaideia*. Remember, it was Paul who said, "We are not ashamed of the Gospel."

Many Christians are genuine and have a real message to impart. But for a message to have any impact, it must be compelling. It must drive the listener to change! The message of the Lord Jesus Christ must persuade the unsaved to make a decision for Christ. It is so important for us to catch the message of *Anagkazo*, biazo and anaideia.

CHAPTER 2

Why Anagkazo is Important

I n the fourteenth chapter of Luke, we read a familiar story where Jesus told of an important person who held a party for his friends. I want you to read this whole portion of Scripture so that you will be familiar with the story.

> Then said he unto him, A certain man made a great supper, and bade many: And sent his servant at supper time to say to them that were bidden, Come; for all things are now ready.
>
> And they all with one consent began to make excuse. The first said unto him, I have bought a piece of ground, and I must needs go and see it: I pray thee have me excused.
>
> And another said, I have bought five yoke of oxen, and I go to prove them: I pray thee have me excused. And another said, I have married a wife, and therefore I cannot come.
>
> So that servant came, and shewed his lord these things. Then the master of the house being angry said to his servant, Go out quickly into the streets and lanes of the city, and bring in hither the poor,

and the maimed, and the halt, and the blind. And the servant said, Lord, it is done as thou hast commanded, and yet there is room.

And the lord said unto the servant, Go out into the highways and hedges, and compel [*anagkazo*] them to come in, that my house may be filled. For I say unto you, That none of those men which were bidden shall taste of my supper.

Luke 14:16-24

This man had the unfortunate experience of spending a lot of money on a big party, inviting important people, only to find out that most of them wouldn't come. This man was very surprised about their rejection of his invitation. He became angry as he listened to the excuses of those he had invited. In his anger, he decided to invite anybody he found on the street.

Imagine having a party with people you don't even know!

Unfortunately, at that time of the night, there were not so many people around. Even after inviting those on the street, his party was relatively unattended. He then decided to invite the sick, the blind and the handicapped. Imagine that! What an unusual selection of partygoers! His party was full of the nonentities and the down-and-outs of society.

Growth through Anagkazo

I believe this story is symbolic of the Lord Jesus sending us out to invite people to Him. It is also symbolic of pastors sending out their members to evangelize the world. I have discovered that every time I embark on evangelizing the world (inviting many people to a great supper), I encounter the same things that this man encountered. However, I believe this man was a success. In spite of everything, he had his party and his house was full of guests. It might not have turned out the way he initially wanted, but he had his party anyway.

You see, God is sending out His church to invite the whole world to know Christ. Unfortunately, many of those who are invited do not respond. The Jews were the first to be invited to know the Lord. But they rejected Christ and the Gospel moved on to the Gentiles.

Many of the elite, who live in large urban centres, hear the Gospel on television and in church. However, they do not receive the message but rather criticize preachers. Again, the Gospel is passed on to the poor and non-elite in villages. They willingly receive the Word because they have no other hope but God.

1. *Anagkazo* **is important because only a certain type of evangelism will lead to church growth.**

People are not going to be convinced or compelled to know God through our little church games. Our "Mickey Mouse" church programmes and bazaars will not go very far in today's world. We must go out there and drive them to God.

2. *Anagkazo* **is important because the people that will fill our empty churches are not in places where they can receive bourgeoisie invitation cards.**

If people are going to be touched with the Gospel, a new strategy of going to the gutters, highways and the bushes must be employed. Sitting in church and inviting people has long been an unworkable strategy for church growth.

3. **Dear pastor, without** *anagkazo*, **your church is going to be empty.**

Please remember that if this man had not employed the strategy of anagkazo he would have had an empty house. Remember this, "A pastor without anagkazo will have an empty church."

4. **Without** *anagkazo,* **many churches are going to die a natural death.**

What you must realize is that the membership of a church is very fluid. Many people come and many people leave. If you don't have more people coming in than those you are losing, your church will begin to die.

If you don't want your church to close down, you must do what Jesus instructed – go out and practise anagkazo.

5. Life is becoming more hectic and people are becoming more busy in the twenty-first century.

Busy working people are going to have more and more excuses. The strategy of anagkazo will help you to overcome these excuses. Through your new driving and forceful attitude you will bring many people to Christ and to church.

CHAPTER 3

How to Practice Anagkazo

1. Use *anagkazo* to prepare a great supper.

Anyone who wants church growth must prepare for it. Most Christian outreaches are not successful unless there is a lot of preparation. Ask yourself how much preparation has gone into anything you do. If there is a lot of preparation there is usually a lot of success. Crusades, church growth, outreaches depend on your preparation. This *anagkazo* man prepared for his great programme.

Being in the ministry has not happened without thousands of hours of preparation. Sermons I preached to ten people some years ago are the same sermons I am preaching to thousands today.

Preaching to a small group of ten people was part of God's preparation for me. If you want God to use you mightily, you must start preparing now! Take every opportunity you have to do something useful in the church.

Years ago, I remember playing the drums and the piano in my church. Though I didn't know it at the time, that was part of my preparation for ministry. Today, I know a lot about music and musical equipment. I can discuss intelligently, all details that concern music, worship and expensive equipment. My experience with the music department has been a valuable asset to me.

2. Use *anagkazo* to influence many people.

You will notice that this man in Luke 14 held a great supper and invited many people. One of the primary reasons churches do not grow is because Christians keep to themselves. You cannot keep to yourself if you want to be an effective witness for the Lord Jesus Christ.

When you sit on a bus, you can decide to be friendly to those nearby. Begin talking to the people around you. I always try to share the Gospel with people around me. I always have some Good News about Jesus. He has saved me and set me free.

During my second year in medical school, we lived on the beautiful Legon campus. We were transported daily to the other side of town where a teaching hospital was located. This involved a one-hour bus drive from one end of town to the other.

Balloons and Condoms

I remember one day as I sat in the bus, I watched some senior colleagues take out condoms, blow them into balloons and fly them in the bus. As these students shouted and laughed over their lewd jokes, I realized how confident they were in what they were doing.

We the Christians sat timidly in the bus, trying to concentrate on our books.

That day, I decided not to keep to myself. I got the attention of everyone on the bus and began to preach. Although preaching on the bus later became quite common, at that time it was unusual. Some of the students were angry and others were bored. Some looked out of the window in disapproval but I preached on! I decided not to keep to myself anymore. I decided to be like the man in Luke 14.

Clapping on the London Bus

An *anagkazo* person does not keep to himself. I once lived in London for a period of time. I felt stifled by the stiff atmosphere in England. I was used to preaching anywhere and everywhere. But in England I couldn't easily relate to the people around. Everyone seemed so unfriendly and uninterested.

One day, while sitting upstairs in a double-decker bus, the spirit of *anagkazo* rose up in me and I said to myself, "I can't keep it to myself any longer."

I rose to my feet and to the surprise of everyone on the bus, I began to clap my hands to get their attention. I tell you, I may have looked bold on the outside, but I was quite scared on the inside.

There were all sorts of murderous looking characters on the bus. But I maintained my cool and delivered a complete Gospel sermon.

The bus was quiet for a few minutes as they listened to this young madman preach. I took my seat after preaching and got off at the next stop. One gentleman, who got off the bus with me said to me, "I admire your courage! But I don't think you got very far." Whether I got very far or not is not what matters. What is important is that I preached the Word. And the Word always accomplishes something when it is preached. ...my word be that goeth forth out of my mouth... it shall accomplish that which I please..." (Isaiah 55:11)

3. **Use *anagkazo* and never cancel your service. Anyone practising *anagkazo* is not prepared to cancel his service.**

Every pastor, in going through the normal processes of church growth, will experience highs and lows. But a pastor with the spirit of *anagkazo* will never cancel his church service. He will decide to press on no matter how many people attend.

One of my pastors told me how only one person attended church on a particular Sunday. He said that he had never felt so low.

However, he managed to preach to that one soul and do his best for the Lord.

Anagkazo in the Community

I remember there was a time we had a very low attendance for one of our services. The Lord told me to do what this man in Luke 14 did: "Go out there and invite the community to church."

I said, "How can I do that on a Sunday?"

The Lord replied, "You do it, and you will be blessed."

I continued arguing with the Lord, "What will our Sunday morning visitors think? We will drive away people from the church."

However, the Lord insisted, "Go out and compel them to come in."

I obeyed the Lord.

I announced to the church that we were going to stop the service, go out into the community and invite them.

I said, "We are going to go out to the community to bring them in."

I announced, "This is not a gentle invitation. Every single one of you must hold the hand of someone you see out there. Physically bring them into the church building."

Some were taken aback. But we did it! And we brought in hundreds of "un-churched" dwellers of the community. That day we had several people giving their lives to Christ. We did this on numerous occasions and over a period, that particular service increased in size dramatically. I was not prepared to close down my service because of a low attendance. That is what any pastor with the spirit of anagkazo is prepared to do.

4. Use *anagkazo* to prevent having empty halls.

A pastor working with the spirit of *anagkazo* is not prepared to have an empty church service. Many years ago, as a medical student, the Lord asked me to start a church. I had no members in my church. Not even one soul to preach to! But I was not prepared to have an empty church.

Anagkazo and the Dawn Broadcast

I was still a student when the Holy Spirit directed me to the nursing students' hostel. I remember that very first day. It was around 5 a.m. and still dark. Standing outside the hostel, I clapped my hands and woke them up. They might have been surprised but that didn't bother me. I preached to them about Jesus. After I had finished I did something very bold. I said to them, "If you want to give your lives to Christ, change out of your night clothes, wear something decent and come downstairs. We want to talk to you about Christ."

That morning several young ladies gave their hearts to God. Up to this day, many of them are still members of my church.

Preaching at dawn to people in their beds has been one of my favourite methods of implementing this principle of *anagkazo*. One morning, I preached at the hostel of public health nurses. A lady threw down a note saying she was a backslider and needed help. She wanted us to speak with her. That morning we ministered to her and God delivered her. She has been a faithful member of our church for the last ten years.

Although I started out with an empty classroom, it soon became filled with nurses who had given their lives to Christ from my *anagkazo* dawn broadcasts.

Dear reader, I want you to understand something; I did not inherit a church from anyone. I have often gone to places where I knew no one, and no one knew me. I have had to go out and win souls, driving and persuading people to the Lord, until the room was full.

5. Use *anagkazo* to overcome people's excuses.

Many people are full of excuses. The man in the story listened to three amazing excuses for not attending his party. However, he was not impressed by any of them.

The first excuse was about testing oxen in the night. Everyone knows that no one tests oxen at that time of the night.

The second excuse was about somebody who had just gotten married. But we all know that a dinner would have been a nice outing for a newly-wed couple.

The third excuse was about going to see some land in the night. Let me ask you a question. Would you not assess a piece of land before you buy it? How could you inspect a piece of land in the night? Would you even see it clearly? Yet somebody was using this as an excuse for not attending the party.

Any good minister, who wants to reach people, must not be overwhelmed by people's excuses. He must learn to overcome people's excuses.

Even as you minister the Word of God, people form excuses in their minds. They develop reasons why they will not obey the Word. Every good preacher must learn to preach against people's excuses and ideas. Jesus spoke directly against the people's reasoning and excuses. And they knew it!

...for they perceived that he had spoken this parable against them.

Luke 20:19

Many excuses cannot be substantiated. A good minister must learn to see through the emptiness of excuses. I spoke to one friend, inviting him to church. He in turn spoke about how the time was not convenient and how he had quite a distance to travel.

I said to him, "You are a successful businessman. Everything you want to do, you do. You travel. You get up early everyday.

You even have time to visit your girlfriend who lives a few hundred kilometres away. How come you have no time for God?"

I told him, "If you really want to do something you can do it."

Some people do not pay their tithes because they claim they have no money. Watch how much money they spend on other things. You will realize that the problem is not a lack of money, but the spirit of greed.

6. Use *anagkazo* to overcome people's lies.

You must learn to overcome the lies and excuses of the people you lead.

I remember once, one of my pastors did some fundraising in a branch church.

During the fundraising, the pastor asked for those who would like to give some money for the purchase of church instruments.

A husband who happened to be a foreigner was prepared to give a donation. Just as his hand was going up, his wife pulled his hand down. She thought the pastor hadn't noticed.

After the service, the lady approached the pastor and said, "You know, the reason why we didn't give any money during the fundraising was because my foreign husband didn't want to give.

She continued, "You know how these foreigners are. They are so stingy."

But that was a lie. It was she who did not want to give anything.

Finally she promised the pastor, "I will see what we can do. I am sure we will be able to help."

All pastors must learn to overcome the lies and excuses of the people we lead.

7. Use *anagkazo* to make a way.

What differentiates the successful from the unsuccessful is the ability to overcome excuses. Notice that the man in Luke 14 was not moved by any of the excuses and reasons given. He made a way out of every circumstance that was produced by the unwilling guests.

I believe in one thing: If you really want to do something you make a way, if you do not want to do something you make an excuse.

They Came to Party

I recall when many young people were unwilling to come to church. The young men especially, made all sorts of excuses. The spirit of *anagkazo* rose up in me and I said, "If they will not come to church, let us have parties for them."

We organized a party for the young people in one area of the city. We made invitation cards and distributed them to the youth in the community. They were very happy and said to themselves, "This is another opportunity to jam."

I remember that evening in particular, we played upbeat Christian music and danced with the unbelievers. One of them told me later that he wondered why they were not being served with beer. At a point in the party, we switched to slower music and stated we had an announcement to make.

By that time, many of the hardened unbelievers were sitting around. To their surprise, I got up and preached the Gospel to them. They were surprised but they still gave their lives to Christ. Many were born again that night.

I have pastors in the church who were saved during some of these surprise evangelistic parties. The Bible says by all means, "save some".

Anagkazo means to *compel* and to *drive* people to God. An anagkazo person is not moved by unfavourable circumstances.

We were not moved by the fact that these young men did not want to attend church. We made a way around that! Learn to make a way where there's no way.

Find a way to overcome every excuse that people place before you.

8.   Use *anagkazo* to go out of your usual circle of friends.

Everyone has a circle of friends. The usual thing is to stay within your circle of friends and acquaintances. However, anyone who wants to be used by God must move out of this regular group. You will notice that the *anagkazo* man in this story was forced to move out of his normal circle of friends. This is a reality that we must face if we want to please God!

I Had My Circle

I had a group of friends I grew up with in Accra. A sort of elitist company made up of the children of foreigners and other bourgeoisie. As a child I travelled first class on intercontinental flights and interacted mainly with the so-called upper echelon of society. I stayed in international cities with my father. My hobbies were swimming and horse riding and horse racing. There were just a few people who had such pastimes.

However, there were hardly any Christians in these circles. When I got born again, I found myself moving out of this circle into a very different group. I moved out into better company, different from what I knew.

The fact is, in order to please God I could not spend a lot of time in those circles anymore. There were simply no believers in that group. If you want to please God you will have to move out of your circle and get to know other groups of people.

I know that the rich man in this story would not normally fellowship with people who live in hedges or who stand on highways.

I know that the rich man in this story would not normally interact with cripples, the blind and the disabled.

However, in order to achieve church growth he had to interact with people of other social backgrounds.

The Nice Little Fellowship Must Grow

I remember in 1984 when I was the leader of a nice fellowship at the university.

We loved each other dearly and were good company for one another (actually, I found my wife in that group). Many of the people that I knew in that little group are still my bosom friends up to this day. However, the Spirit of God impressed upon me to move out of our little group and to go to people we didn't know.

I remember some people were not in favour of expanding our nice little clique.

"If you bring in more people, we will lose something," they said. "There's something about a small fellowship. It's nice to be petite. It's a cute little family."

But I led this group into one outreach after another, driving and necessitating people to come to the Lord. I was never tired of preaching. People are not tired of sinning, why should you be tired of spreading the gospel?

During the second year of the medical school (which by the way is the most difficult year), I led this group in dawn broadcasts every Saturday morning. Everyone knew about us. They were used to our voices that rang out loud and clear every Saturday morning.

"Thank God for our nice little fellowship," I said. "But we have to go out there and win souls." We must move out of our little circle.

After awhile, unbelievers are no longer impressed with our sermons. If you do not rise up with a new approach, a new *anagkazo* method, your message will lose its punch.

As we continued preaching at dawn, I realized that people just turned over in their beds and ignored us. I said to myself, "Our messages are no longer driving people to the Lord."

But the Spirit of the Lord gave me a bright idea.

Knock on Their Doors!

Since the people were now so used to our voices, we needed to do something new. I decided to send out a group to stand outside the doors of their rooms.

I told the preacher for the morning, "When you get to the altar call, we will start knocking on their doors."

I told him, "Tell the people who are listening to you that they are going to hear a knock on their door. If they want to accept Christ they should open up and we will come in and lead them to the Lord."

The preacher followed my instructions. Suddenly, those who were ignoring us had to pay attention. We were knocking on their doors at 5 a.m.! Believe me, many were gloriously born again during those morning broadcasts.

Salvation for the Mocker

I vividly remember one brother in particular; He would laugh at Christians as they spoke in tongues. He made fun of the gift of speaking in tongues. This is someone who would get drunk and lie by one of the many ponds scattered around the beautiful campus of the University of Ghana. That morning as my friend the evangelist preached and said, "Perhaps you are hearing a knock on your door. If you want to be born again open your door and someone will come in and lead you to the Lord", I happened to knock on the door of this young man.

I was surprised when he opened the door and welcomed us in. He said, "I knew you would come here. Today is my day!" We prayed with him and he gave his heart to the Lord that very morning. To this day, this man is serving the Lord. I give glory to God for all the people that have been born again as we have forcefully moved out to speak the Word. *Anagkazo* works!

9. Use *anagkazo* as long as there is room in your church.

    ...and yet there is room.

                                                    Luke 14:22

A song that I love goes like this: *There's room at the cross for you. There's room at the cross for you. Though millions have come, there's still room for one. There's room at the cross for you.*

Do not be satisfied as long as there is room in your church. The man in this story sent out his servants simply because there was room.

I believe that every church should arrange more chairs than the people who actually come. The presence of empty pews should motivate the pastor to reach out until the house is full. The whole essence of church growth is to have a full church.

...compel [*anagkazo*] them to come in, that my house may be filled.

Luke 14:23

Evangelism is directly related to church growth. All our efforts to lead people to the Lord should bear fruit. We must see our efforts filling church buildings.

Whatever the case, a minister must see that there is room at the cross for one more soul. I believe that if we have this mind, God will use us to fill the church.

I have never been satisfied with the size of my church. When we had ten people, I wanted twenty. When we had fifty, I dreamed of a hundred. When God gave me one hundred people, I thought to myself, "What would it be like if I had five hundred people?" When the church was numbered in the hundreds, I thought, "What would it be like if we had thousands?"

I think a pastor will get tired of preaching to the same few people after awhile. We must be motivated to have a fuller house. These words keep ringing in my soul, "That my house may be filled!" "That my house may be filled!" Dear Pastor, never forget that there is still room at the cross.

CHAPTER 4

How to Practice Anaideia and Biazo

Anaideia and biazo are the keys to being a good Christian. Anaideia and biazo are the keys to church growth. Evangelism is the key to getting new people to join your church. Without biazo and anaideia you will never evangelise effectively.

Biazo

Verily I say unto you, among them that are born of women there hath not risen a greater than John the Baptist: notwithstanding he that is least in the kingdom of heaven is greater than he. And from the days of John the Baptist until now the kingdom of heaven suffereth violence, and the violent [biazo] take it by force.

Matthew 11:11,12

Multitudes of non-Christians are hurtling down a broad street to Hell. They sing, they dance, and they wine and dine. They do not give a hoot about the Gospel we preach! Many of us Christians live in our nice little world where we are oblivious to the reality of sinners going to Hell.

I once worked as a sub-intern at the mortuary of the largest hospital in Ghana. Something struck me that I want to share with you. Every few minutes a car would park outside the mortuary. In that car was the body of a man sprawled in the back seat, or even sometimes in the boot (trunk).

I would stand at the main door of the mortuary as people brought in their loved ones and relatives who had died at home or on the street. These people were so sad and shaken. You must understand that only a few hours earlier they had been talking to a living person who was now gone forever. They were bringing their loved one to a fridge.

I noticed that there did not seem to be any particular time of the day when dead people were brought to this mortuary. As I stood there, God showed me that people were dying across the city all the time. Death is not reserved for early mornings or late nights. It happens anytime and anywhere.

A person who has never stood at the door of a mortuary will not know how common death is. How frequently people depart for eternity! Just as the Lord spoke to his prophets when they saw certain things, the Lord spoke to me when I stood at that door. He asked, "How many of these people do you think were saved?"

"I died for them; I gave up my life for them, but are they saved?"

Listen to me Christian friend. Our church bazaars, weddings, fellowships and nice choirs are not enough to win the multitudes to Christ. People are hurtling down the road of destruction. They do not even know that they are going to Hell.

Don't Let Them Ignore Your Message

They Heard the Music

This reminds me of the Second World War in which the prisoners were taken to large camps. They were stripped of their clothes and herded into huge gas chambers. As they filed in, their captors would play beautiful music for the prisoners. They heard the music. How soothing and refreshing it must have sounded. "Surely nothing evil is going to happen to us," they thought. Little did they know that they were about to be slaughtered by the same people who were playing the music.

This is the lot of unbelievers today. They hear the music of the devil. The melodies and lullabies of this present world charm them. Because of these things, they do not know that they are walking to their own destruction. "...as an ox goeth to the slaughter..." (Proverbs 7:22).

In Matthew 11:12, the Bible tells us that the violent take the kingdom of God by force. What does this mean?

The Twentieth Century New Testament puts it this way, **...men using force have been seizing it...**

The William's Translation says, **...men are seizing it as a precious prize...**

The Goodspeed translation says, **...Men have been taking the kingdom of heaven by storm...**

The Weymouth translation says, **...the kingdom of God has been enduring violent assault...**

All these Scriptures tell us one thing. Gentle words, nice songs, lame sermons and docile choirs cannot help much in this indifferent and uninterested world. People don't want to know. They are deceived.

Church Games Will Not Help

They don't care whether Jesus comes today or tomorrow. "Leave me alone," they say. "To Hell with this church business of yours."

That is why we need what the Bible calls *biazo*. *Biazo* means to use force and to force one's way into a thing. Many people are blinded by the devil. We must open their eyes to the realities of Heaven and Hell.

...the god of this world hath blinded the minds of them...

2 Corinthians 4:4

Apostle Paul did not only give nice sermons. He was actively involved in turning the heads and opening the eyes of unbelievers.

I always know when people are ignoring the message. But I don't want anybody to ignore this important message – I must turn their heads and open their eyes. One particular morning, my group in the university found ourselves in a hall, preaching.

I Called out Their Room Numbers

I realized that the young ladies (it was a ladies' hall) were just turning over in their beds, some with their boyfriends. They knew that we would end our "disturbance" after a short while. The Spirit of God gave me a quick instruction on how to use *biazo* on that occasion.

He whispered, "Do not preach generally, but call out their room numbers and direct the preaching to individual rooms."

I obeyed.

They Were Shocked to Hear Their Room Numbers

I gave each of the dawn broadcasters four or five rooms to preach to. It was an amazing experience! The people were so surprised to hear their room numbers being mentioned. A voice was coming out in the darkness speaking very specifically to the occupants of particular rooms.

Everyone knew they were being addressed personally by God. Of course, some of them were very angry.

And some had their boyfriends sleeping in their rooms with them. They could not help but hear a personal and direct message.

I remember that in response to this one lady ran out of her room, came downstairs, lifted up her hands and said, "I want to give my life to Christ today! I want to be born again!"

Some were outraged, but some were saved. The Bible says,

...blessed is he, whosoever shall not be offended in me.

Matthew 11:6

Don't Preach to Yourself!

When we have city-wide crusades, I stand on the platform and command my church members to go out into the community. We don't wait for them to come to us; we go out there and bring them from their homes.

One day, we even went to a "Red Light District" and brought a group of prostitutes to the crusade. I was very happy to see these prostitutes coming to the altar to give their lives to the Lord. You see, if we hadn't forced these women out of their "work places" and to the crusade, they would never have been saved. Most prostitutes do not go to church. They would have just gone about their daily routine. We would have ended up preaching to ourselves.

Christian friends, let's stop playing games. If we are going to preach the Gospel, let's not preach to ourselves. Let's go out there and drive them in (*anagkazo* and *biazo*) to the Lord.

Anaideia

I say unto you, Though he will not rise and give him, because he is his friend, yet because of his importunity [*anaideia*] he will rise and give him as many as he needeth.

Luke 11:8

In Luke 11, Jesus told us a story of a man who needed three loaves of bread. This man buried his shame and embarrassment and went to his friend's house at a very odd hour. The master of the house was woken up.

He might have shouted, "What is happening? Are there some armed robbers here? Is there a fire? What is going on outside?"

The servant of the house probably replied, "It's the neighbour. He says he wants some bread for his visitors."

Dear Christian friend, most of us would not disturb even our best friends at midnight. How much more to ask for something trivial like bread!

But Jesus' message here is very simple. If you are ashamed to press for certain things, you will never achieve them. If you are shameless in trying to achieve church growth you will accomplish things that others will only dream about! God has shown me that people who are very concerned about their public image cannot achieve much for God.

Are You Ashamed of the Work of God?

It takes anaideia, shamelessness, to start a church. When I discussed with my friend the idea of starting a church, I remember he looked at me in amazement. He said, "What if people don't come to the church? We will be so embarrassed. People in town will hear that we tried to start a church that didn't work."

By starting a church, I don't mean to break away with a large segment of someone else's ministry. I am talking about moving into a room that has two or three people and preaching to them. It takes shamelessness to tell these few people that they are now in a great church. If you are not prepared to go through the shame and ridicule of standing in an empty room and looking odd, you will never achieve great things for God.

Are You Ashamed?

One pastor told me he was afraid to do an altar call (inviting people to give their life to Christ). What if no one responds? Would you not feel ashamed? People will think that you are not anointed and that your message was not powerful enough. It is this very train-of-thought that keeps people away from powerful ministry.

One of my Elders called and told me that for the first time someone in the church had responded to her altar call. You see, she had been shamelessly doing altar calls with no one responding. But with *anaideia* (shamelessness and persistence) she eventually had results!

Are You Ashamed of the Healing Ministry?

The shameless man, who asked for the bread, eventually accomplished his goal. I remember when I first began to pray for the sick. I was very worried about what people would think about me.

Many times whilst standing on stage, the devil would tell me, "Don't even bother to call out for testimonies; no one will be healed."

The devil told me, "Do not disgrace yourself any further. Just end the service here and send the people home."

But the Spirit of the Lord rose up within me and I said to myself, "I am not ashamed. If no one gets healed this time, I will do it again, and again, and again! One day, someone will get healed." I am glad to say that many have been healed.

After I had qualified from the medical school, I worked for one year as a medical doctor.

Are You Ashamed of Full-Time Ministry?

At a point, the Lord began to speak to me about entering full-time ministry. I argued with the Lord, "I will work and bring enough money to support the church."

I continued, "What will people think of me, leaving such a noble profession to enter such a controversial one." I told the Lord, "No one knows my church! And no one knows me!"

"Worst of all, what a shame it is for me to live off people's offerings."

"That's ridiculous! Why should people contribute their pennies for my upkeep? I find it degrading," I thought.

However, the Lord told me, "They that preach the Gospel must live off the Gospel."

Even so hath the Lord ordained that they which preach the gospel should live of the gospel.

1 Corinthians 9:14

I had to bury my pride as a doctor and shamelessly enter full-time ministry. Through the revelation of shamelessness (*anaideia*), I have been able to work in the ministry. Through shamelessness, I have overcome the laughter and mockery of my detractors.

[77]*Anaideia* (shamelessness) is the key you need to accomplish great things for God!